My Foster Parents

AUTHOR DR. JAMILLAH SMITH

AuthorHouse™
1663 Liberty Drive
Bloomington, IN 47403
www.authorhouse.com
Phone: 833-262-8899

Because of the dynamic nature of the Internet, any web addresses or links contained in this book may have changed since publication and may no longer be valid. The views expressed in this work are solely those of the author and do not necessarily reflect the views of the publisher, and the publisher hereby disclaims any responsibility for them.

Any people depicted in stock imagery provided by Getty Images are models, and such images are being used for illustrative purposes only.
Certain stock imagery © Getty Images.

This book is printed on acid-free paper.

ISBN: 978-1-6655-3835-0 (sc)
ISBN: 978-1-6655-3836-7 (e)

Print information available on the last page.

Published by AuthorHouse 03/30/2022

author HOUSE®

About This Book

This book is about a young girl name Josie. Josie lives with Mr. and Mrs. Brown. In this book, you will read how Josie copes with transitioning into her new family, home, and school.

Hello! My name is Josie. Mr. and Mrs. Brown are my foster parents.

My foster parents are the best.
They offer me so much love
and care. We eat breakfast,
lunch, and dinner just to have
our special time together.

Here is my new home. My foster parents welcome me into their home. Yippee! I am so happy.

Home is where I relax and feel safe. Mr. and Mrs. Brown invite their families to celebrate birthdays and holidays. I enjoy the special times we spend together as a family.

Here is my bedroom.

I have a beautiful room. My bedroom is very colorful. My favorite colors are white, pink, and purple. This is where I sleep and read my favorite book.

Here are my friends.

My friend's names are Rosa, Barry, Timothy, and Sara. My friends and I live on the same street. We play jump rope, hide, and seek, and do homework together after school.

Here is my new school. I have new teachers and classmates.

My teachers and classmates are great. My favorite subject is science. In math, we learn about math symbols. These symbols help me know when to add or subtract. In science, I learned about the solar system.

When you are sad, do your favorite things. I guarantee you will be happy and have a smile on your face.

Look at me!

Whenever I am feeling sad or missing my family and old friends, here is what I love to do that makes me happy.

- Read my favorite book.

- Play with my new friends outside.

- Spend time with Mr. and Mrs. Brown.

- Draw pictures or doodle.

When I am overwhelmed with school, my foster parents would help me with my schoolwork. They always remind me, "we are here to help and support you."

When you are feeling sad or just having a bad day, remember me, Josie! God will take care of you and so will your foster parents.

Hello! We are Josie's foster parents. Like Josie, you may feel overwhelmed with your new changes. Remember, your foster parents are there for you. They want to offer you the best love, care, and guidance.

The End

About the Author

Hello! My name is Jamillah Smith. I was born and raised in New Jersey. Currently, I live in North Carolina. I have a BA in Education, MA in Supervision and Administration, and Doctorate in Educational Leadership. I have been teaching for over 17 years. When I was a young girl, I've experienced transitioning into my foster parent's home. It was not easy. I wrote this book to help children who are struggling with transitioning into their foster parent's home.

Dr. Jamillah Smith

- Must get permission to copyright. Copyright2021

Printed in the United States
by Baker & Taylor Publisher Services